THOUGHTS
FOR TROUBLED TIMES

THOUGHTS AND PRAYERS FOR TROUBLED TIMES

Lionel Fanthorpe

BISHOPSGATE PRESS

© 1989 Lionel Fanthorpe

British Library Cataloguing in Publication Data
Fanthorpe, Lionel
Thoughts and prayers for troubled times.
1. Christian life. Prayers - Devotional works
I. Title
242′ .8

ISBN 1-85219-027-2

All enquiries and requests relevant to this title should be sent to the publisher, Bishopsgate Press Ltd., 37 Union Street, London SE1 1SE

Printed by Whitstable Litho Printers Ltd., Millstrood Road, Whitstable, Kent

Alphabetical List of Topics

Foreword

"Yet man is born unto trouble as the sparks fly up-ward." Job, long years ago, was speaking from his own experience, but many, down the centuries, will always re-echo his words. Into some sad lives troubles press very hard and persist with their pain and disappointment.

Of course, some of our troubles we bring on ourselves. They are to some extent largely self-inflicted wounds. Lewis Carroll in his "Alice Through the Looking-glass" pokes his usual gentle fun at the antics of his White Knight, making his laborious way through life with self-imposed burdens, carrying wherever he went a large mousetrap because of his fear of mice, a beehive lest he lose the chance of gathering the honey he so enjoyed, knives at the ankles of his horse to save both horse and rider from the presence of sharks, and to cap it all, a large empty meat dish on which he was always hoping someone would place his favourite plum cake. With the weight of his armour, and what he carried, his was a very laboured way through life. All the White Knight had to do to free himself from his burdens was to put them down. That is how it goes in Wonderland!

In real life it is not so easy to be free of our burdens. They become part of us; they may be ours for life; we have somehow to learn to identify them, to understand their capacity to hurt, to live with them as graciously as we can, with the least harm to those around us, and in our darker moments, when our own resources crumble, to know where to turn for help.

The author of this small book I first came to know as

the Headmaster of a Comprehensive school and an active member of his local Parish Church. He is now a Priest of the Church and it was my privilege to serve as one of his tutors on his way to Ordination to the Non-Stipendiary Ministry. He remains Headmaster of his school, but it is as a Priest he has written this book. It is the work of a caring, perceptive compassionate man, with a wide experience of life with its fluctuations to good or ill, and with an obvious love of people of all ages and in all conditions. His skill as a writer has been proved over the years by the many books he has written. His facility in writing and his command of language are gifts for us lesser mortals to admire. In this book he writes not so much as an author, skilled in his craft, but as a Priest, with deep understanding of the people he has been Ordained to serve. He is anxious to comfort where he can, to share the Faith he has found with those who may despair of their own. The book will be a source of hope and comfort to many in the years that lie ahead.

Every tutor knows that those pupils who needed assistance least are generally those who acknowledge most generously the help they were given. Lionel Fanthorpe has been kind enough to say that I was of use to him on his way to Ordination, and he has twice asked me to write a Foreword for his books. If I helped at all I am proud to have served him; but I also owe much to him for, of course, among the first, I have read this book. Many others will find new strength and hope from it. The power of God is in the writer and now dominates this book.

Canon Stanley Mogford,
Cardiff

Introduction

It is part of human nature to be far more acutely aware of a small problem that affects us directly and personally than of a massive disaster from which we are comfortably insulated by space and time.

Objective historians would probably concede that no period of history has ever been completely peaceful or trouble free. The most experienced traveller would tell us that although some parts of the earth are much more peaceful and pleasant than others, he has been nowhere which was totally free of difficulties.

Then there are individual differences to take into account. Some hypersensitive people seem to be more put out by a broken nail than others are by a broken arm. One man is less concerned about a bullet wound than another is about a raspberry thorn in his finger.

How then can we define *trouble* in any useful or practical way that will have some sort of general application?

The following basic rules may help a little:—

1. Take account of what the trouble means to the one who is enduring it. A wasp-sting may be only a trivial nuisance to you; it can be a source of real agony and terror to some sensitive people. Listen sensitively to how the victim feels about his problem.

2. Ask whom the trouble affects: will it have repercussions for the victim's immediately family and friends only, or will it go wider and deeper than that?

Will it harm the town, the county, the nation, or half a continent?

3. Is it a problem of body, mind or spirit — or perhaps of all three? Is it an illness or an injury with physical consequences? Is it a load of guilt, anxiety, emotional distress or depression that torments the mind? Is it some sinister evil that oppresses the spirit, dragging it down, seeking to separate it from the love of Christ, seeking to erect a barrier between the sinner and his God?

4. From what perspective is it being viewed? This morning's problems are huge, tonight's are vast, tomorrow's are gigantic; next week's are a little smaller, and next month's seem almost manageable. As for next year and the year after ... Why, things might almost be trouble free! My difficulty with a colleague at work seems insurmountable when I am in the office with him and the atmosphere is electric with the tension between us. As I drive home, the problem remains grave but is not totally impossible. By the time I'm having supper with the family, I'm beginning to wonder why I felt quite so tense about things in the office. After watching a good video and giving the dog his late night walk I can see that it wasn't really much of a problem at all and I wonder why I let it get to me at the time. Seen from the vantage point of a starving refugee in Ethiopia, whether Smith or Jones won the promotion to Clerical Officer Grade II, which both felt entitled to, is trivial and inconsequential in the extreme. If Smith is left a six-figure legacy, or learns that he is terminally ill, the promotion to Clerical Officer Grade II loses almost all its impact.

Having tried to think for a few minutes about what we mean by *trouble,* how can we best deal with our own? Again, four basic principles may be of help:—

1. Are we standing too close to it? Are we being too sensitive to it? Will it seem as important next week as we think it is at this moment?

2. Will it really have any consequences worth speaking of outside of my own thoughts and feelings? Will my village or my valley be any the worse for it? Will it damage my family or friends in any way? If its effects are strictly limited to what it can do to me, then is it, perhaps, not half as important as I felt it was when I first started worrying about it?

3. Does this difficulty affect my body, my mind, my spirit or some combination of all three? Is a problem in one part of our being spilling over and contaminating the rest? Can we take some simple, practical action to put it right? Perhaps my Priest or my Pastor can help me in my search for peace with God, or advise me on some ethical or moral dilemma which I'm feeling unhappy and guilty about. My dental surgeon can do something about the toothache that's been dominating everything else in my life since Friday evening. My GP can reassure me that symptoms I've been worrying about for a month are caused by something perfectly harmless and easily treatable.

4. Can I make a really strenuous effort to change my perspective, and, with God's help, succeed? My own troubles are tiny, sharp-sided grains of sand in my eyes. My neighbour's troubles are vast boulders; but locked inside the prison of my own selfishness, those

11

boulders are many miles away. I can hardly see them, let alone help him to lift them. Curiously enough, though, when I do occasionally manage to struggle briefly out of my all-enveloping, incarcerating selfishness, and try to lift one corner of his boulder to help him, I seem to lose for a time the painful irritant of the grit in my own eyes.

Trouble is susceptible to being shared; it is highly vulnerable to fellowship. Share it with a loving family and good friends and companions here on earth, and it is weakened to the point where it is bearable. Take it to God: share it with Christ; and it becomes imperceptible.

In this all too frequently sad, dangerous and bewildering world in which we live, troubles seem to come in many different forms and guises: in the pages which follow I have attempted to suggest some thoughts and prayers which may be of some small comfort on some of these occasions.

My personal prayer for you is that whatever your problems and difficulties you may always have the Grace to turn to Almighty God, our Heavenly Father, and to His only son, Jesus Christ our Lord and Saviour. In Him, I know you will find everlasting joy and eternal peace. God Bless you, heal you, protect and preserve you, now and forever more. Amen.

Lionel Fanthorpe, Cardiff, 1988

Accident

Thoughts

The world is a wonderful and exciting place, but it is also a dangerous and terrifying place. The exhilarating joys and thrills of speed turn all too easily into tragedy and terrible injury.

The quiet safety of our houses is filled with the hidden dangers of gas and electricity. The homely pan or kettle can give an agonising and disabling scald if upset. The lawn-mower or the power saw can cut flesh and bone as easily as grass and timber.

We must always exercise great care, especially when others depend upon us, or when what we are doing can injure them if we make a mistake, or slip. Safety is a Christian duty, part of our responsibility to our neighbours.

Many accidents can be prevented if we think enough and care enough.

Accidents have always raised questions in people's minds: questions about the cause. How could God let it happen? Was it some form of divine judgement? Jesus answers at least one of those persistent questions when He talks about the Tower of Siloam which fell and killed a number of people. "They were not greater sinners than the rest of you," He assured his hearers. It is only insurance underwriters who refer to 'Acts of God' in that sense! Jesus has taught us better. An accident is a salutary reminder to us all that this life is neither secure nor permanent, even when it lulls us into a sense of false security. Metaphorically speaking we are all standing dangerously close to the Tower of Siloam. We are all much closer to eternity than we realise. Are we ready to meet our Maker? Have we accepted Christ's forgiveness? Are we cleansed from all sin by the power of his Blood?

An accident is not something that only happens to other people. Nothing in this world matters except being right with God, and expressing our love for Christ by loving the men and women for whom He died. If we are sure about Him, we have nothing to fear and all things to hope for.

Prayers

For All of Us

Almighty and most merciful God, Maker and Sustainer of this great and mysterious universe in which we live, but which we comprehend only in part, help us to understand what our Lord Jesus meant when he spoke of the Tower of Siloam. Give us such knowledge of Your Creation and its laws that all groundless fears and futile superstitions are driven from our minds. Help us to see that those who suffer accident and misfortune are neither better nor worse than the rest of us. Help us never to try to blame You, our loving Father, for accidents that arise from human ignorance, foolishness, impatience or carelessness. Grant us the grace to help those who suffer as a result of accidents, to do all we can to prevent them, and to pray for Your protection for all whose lives bring them into peril and danger, on land, on sea and in the skies. We ask it for the sake of Jesus Christ our Saviour, who gave His very life that we might live, and taught us that in being willing to risk our earthly lives for Him and for mankind, we are gaining life eternal. Amen.

For Accident Victims

Lord bless, protect and help all accident victims. Let them not be embittered or alienated by their suffering and loss, but find You, the Suffering Saviour, in their own pain and distress. Heal and restore them, Lord, as you raised up the lame, gave hearing to the deaf, and sight to the blind in Galilee when You walked on earth with men. We ask it in and through Your precious Name. Amen.

For Ourselves

Help me, my family and friends, Almighty Father, as we suffer because of this accident that has happened to me. Help us to understand its true significance and meaning, and not to be driven from You because of it. Bring joy from pain, strength from weakness, courage and confidence from fear and bewilderment. Help us to rebuild our broken lives and to go on again with Your Holy Spirit to comfort and guide us, for the sake of Christ our Lord. Amen.

Alcohol and Drug Abuse

Thoughts

The alcoholic and the drug addict are trying to escape.

They have found life too difficult, or meaningless, or frightening, or boring; or perhaps something has happened to them that has made life too tragic or too horrible to cope with.

Some may have begun as adventurers looking for new and exciting experiences, not realising that all drugs and alcohol had to offer them was addiction, illness and ultimately death.

The worst of their tragedy is that they were right to feel dissatisfied: their fatal error was to seek for the cure in the wrong places. There is no real meaning to life except in Christ. Everything else, however interesting and absorbing at the start cannot satisfy us. Man has a hunger and thirst for God which only God can satisfy. One of the dark ironies of the drug and alcohol problem is that men and women who are subconsciously seeking the Highest can be dragged down to the lowest.

Prayer

Almighty and Everlasting God, have mercy on those who set out to find an answer to their emptiness of spirit, and found only ruin and tragedy. Put new life and strength of will into those whose wills have been enslaved by alcohol and drugs. Set their weary feet upon the road that leads to You. Help Your servants to help them and to sympathise with them, that we may be signposts and milestones along the road that leads them back to Christ. Help all those medical and social workers who specialise in the care of the addict and the alcoholic, that they may have skill, courage, wisdom, kindness and patience. We ask it in and through the Name of Christ our Lord. Amen.

———————————

Alone

Thoughts

God did not make us to be alone.

Man needs fellowship: with God and with other human beings.

A flock of birds, a shoal of fish, an ocean of waves, a family of people, God's family the Church: our need of one another is so great that good companionship is a condition of life.

In our sin and stupidity we try to shut ourselves away from God and from one another. It is as mindless as trying to hold our breath and do without air. It is a social version of anorexia nervosa, a morbid starvation of our natural and healthy desire to be with God and with His other children. It is as if a man decided that drinking pure, clear, sparkling water will not quench his thirst. He is aware of the thirst, and he may also have a strong suspicion that unless he does something about it, it will eventually be fatal to him: yet he cannot bring himself to admit that what he needs is water.

We find it desperately hard to turn to God and our fellow men for company even when we are painfully aware that loneliness is destroying a vital part of us.

The worst kinds of loneliness are often self-inflicted. We are not so often shut off by physical and social barriers from the good companions God has given us, as by work pressures and distances, as by something inside ourselves which gets its priorities wrong. It is as though we dislike getting into real, meaningful, committed contact with our fellow beings more than we dislike the loneliness which is making us miserable. Worse still, it is as though we sometimes deliberately hold back from coming to seek our Heavenly Father Himself, apparently preferring the sadness and emptiness of being alone to the warmth and joy of being with the Ultimate Companion.

It is only when we put fellowship with Him first that we can overcome both kinds of loneliness: the terrible emptiness of enforced loneliness, the kind that is not of our making and not of our choosing; and the selfish loneliness which our pride and ego-centredness inflict upon us.

Prayer

Almighty Father, Eternal Son and Ever-loving Spirit, Immortal Trinity of Perfect Union and Harmony, help us to defeat our loneliness. Lord of all Blessed Communion, so often we do not understand what ails us; help us to see that it is deliberate breaking of fellowship, and the ruthless seeking of our own selfish ends that so often leads to loneliness. Help us, Lord, to recognize our need of fellowship with You and with our brothers and sisters on earth, and to act towards them in goodness and love. Deliver us, Lord of Hosts, from the loneliness which is not our fault. Change and improve all circumstances and situations which isolate and separate us; bring loving arms of fellowship to find us, and bring us and all whom we love to Your Eternal Kingdom where we shall never know loneliness again, for the sake of Him who founded the holy fellowship of the Church, and sealed it with His precious blood, Jesus Christ our Lord. Amen.

Anxiety

Thoughts

Anxiety belongs to the same unwholesome, unhealthy and unwelcome tribe as worry and stress, but although there are marked family likenesses, there are also individual characteristics which make each one unpleasantly unique and specific.

Anxiety is that uneasy feeling we all have from time to time that there is something to worry about, that there is something in the vicinity which is capable of generating stress. Anxiety is the shapeless aspect of worry. It is the amorphous, nebulous cloud in which the stress-generator is concealed. We can feel anxious without really knowing what we are getting anxious *about*. It is a crippling thing. Pulses race; hearts beat faster, but in an unpleasant way; we feel tense and irritable; we think we hear sounds in the silent emptiness of a dark street or a deserted house. We imagine that we see sinister shapes and furtive shadows where they have no right to be. The less we know about the real or imagined danger, the more anxious we become, and the less capable of acting. Anxiety is a paralysing agent. It is a mind-parasite: we cannot think or plan in the grip of high anxiety because it absorbs so much of our mental energy.

Anxiety is dispelled by faith, dissolved by love, destroyed by that child-like trust in God our Father which Jesus Himself always advocated. The same human mind cannot be filled with that simple trust and with anxiety at the same time. Why do we allow ourselves to feel anxious so often when God loves us so much and cares so wonderfully for us?

Prayer

Most caring, loving and protecting Lord, forgive me for my foolish anxieties. I know that they are wrong. I know that they act as a barrier between me and the joy that you wish me and all your children to share forever. Dear Lord, You made me and You know my every weakness: the things of this world that frighten me and make me anxious often seem so close, while the things of Heaven seem so distant. When I am afraid help me to feel Your Presence; when I am anxious, teach me to trust more deeply; when the future looks dark and threatening help me to see the Light of Christ; when I am tense and nervous grant me that peace which the world cannot give, for the sake of Him who died and rose again to bring it, Jesus Christ our Lord. Amen.

Bereavement

Thoughts

The souls of the righteous are in the hands of God. Hold on to that. It is true. It is relevant.

Parting with someone we love is an agony beyond description, and only God can help us to endure it.

What form does that help take?

Firstly, He reassures us in Scripture, in the teachings of the Church, and above all in the work and witness of His Son, Jesus Christ, that death is not the end. Christ, our great Warrior Priest, has conquered death, has burst open the gates of hell and set the prisoners free. Death has no more dominion. It is an agonising illusion, but no more than an illusion. When children watch horror films (to which they should not have been admitted!) they are terrified of what they see on the screen. They are frightened and dismayed by moving shapes and colours on a white wall. The actors who made the film are many miles away doing something completely different. The characters on the screen are only imaginary, the creation of the film-writer's mind. The actors who played the parts are just ordinary men and women like us. They are neither horrible nor frightening. The monsters are made of plastic and rubber. Often they are tiny figures only a few centimetres high, enlarged by clever trick photography. It is a terrifying experience to watch that film, but it is *unreal*.

The Ultimate Truth at the back of this mysterious and

wonderful universe is that God our Father loves us more than we can understand now, limited as we are here by time and space. He wants us, and our loved ones, to be happy with Him and with one another forever. He is good enough and powerful enough to make that happen. Trust Him. It will all come right in the End, because God is the End, and God is love. He cares far, far more for the loved one we have lost than we do. No harm can come to him, or to her, in the hands of our loving Father. All shall be well. We shall be re-united. All the love we have known on this earth, has been shadowed by the unspoken fear that those we love will die one day, and we shall lose them. There are some poor souls who have never dared to love with all their hearts because they could not bear the thought of losing the one they love so much. When we are re-united in Heaven, we shall all dare to love with the whole of our enriched being because we shall know that there is no more death, and our love for one another in Heaven brings joy unshadowed by the nameless dread.

Prayer

Lord, You wept for Lazarus, Your friend, and cried over Jerusalem. Take pity on our grief, O Lord of tears and joy, and comfort us. Give us the inward assurance that those we love who have left this world are safe with You, and even now experiencing a joy beyond our understanding. Grant them safe lodging and places at Your Everlasting Feast. Re-unite us all one day, O loving Lord, that together again eternally, we may worship You in glory, forever and forever. Amen.

Crime

Thoughts

One famous criminologist is on record as saying that the quickest way to abolish crime would be to abolish the law. If there were no laws to break, there could be no criminals. The disadvantage of such a scheme, of course, is that the comment in Hobbes' *Leviathan* would be horribly apposite, and the life of man under such anarchic conditions would be "poor, nasty, brutish and *short*."

We need, however, to be equally clear about the essential differences between law-breaking, crime and sin. I may break some minor point of civil law by parking in the wrong place, or in the right place for ten minutes too long. If I break into my neighbour's house and remove his camera, video-recorder, and assorted jewellery belonging to his wife, I am committing a crime. In this latter case the crime is a sin as well, as it infringes the Law of God as well as the laws of the United Kingdom.

If we transgress God's Law against adultery, we are not committing a crime under the British Law, although it would be considered so in some Moslem States, but we are committing a sin.

We need to keep these differences clearly before us as we think about the laws of man, the Law of God, crime and sin.

It may be very comforting and convenient for those who favour such phrases as "situational ethics" and words like "pragmatism" and "expediency" to argue against the existence of an absolute, eternal and unchanging moral code. But morality and ethics do not change at the whim of that curious, fickle and unreliable deity "the spirit of the age". According to some of his worshippers, morality is no more than a function of fashion, and ethics a subtle and palate pleasing wine miraculously and instantaneously brewed from anything convenient and contemporary.

Law, order, decency, authority and good, strong discipline are anathema to our sick modern society, yet they are the medicines it most desperately needs if it is to recover.

Human laws at their best are based upon the timeless and changeless Law of God, that same Law which Christ Himself came not to set aside but to fulfil. But this timeless and priceless Law must be written in men's hearts, not just in their legal codes; and it is only our Lord Jesus Christ who can write it there, and give us grace to live by what He has written.

Prayers

Almighty Giver of Perfect and Timeless Law, Judge of all men, and Fountain Head of all that is fair, honest and true, have mercy upon our sin, our weakness and our crime. Forgive us for breaking Your Divine Law, and for setting aside your holy and unchanging precepts. Write Your Law afresh in every penitent heart, and give us the strength and grace to keep it, through Jesus Christ, our Lord. Amen.

Lord of Mercy, welcoming and forgiving Father, help and guide all those who have gone astray and become criminals. Assist them by the power of Your Holy Spirit to find their way safely home to Your throne of mercy. Assist them to repent and begin their lives anew in the power of Christ. Help us to welcome back into fellowship, with warmth and Christian love, all those who have come to themselves as did the prodigal son in the alien land, and turned again to the Father's love. Ever remind us, Lord, that but for Your grace, we might well have been far worse than they, our sins and crimes more loathsome in Your sight. Teach us never to judge, never to condemn, but only to give thanks and rejoice when a sinner repents, through Jesus Christ our Lord. Amen.

Lord of all valour and courage, be with those who uphold the law and protect us from crime and danger. Help the Police, the Security Services, and all who keep watch over us. Let them be brave, impartial and fair; discerning, thoughtful, and honest in the fulfilment of their duty. May those who protect us themselves be under Your protection, and may they find satisfaction and peace of mind in a job well done. We ask it in the Name of the Good Shepherd who gave His life to protect His sheep, Jesus Christ our Lord. Amen.

Cruelty

Thoughts

It was Shakespeare who most poignantly highlighted man's inhumanity to man, and Christ who most clearly taught the need for brotherly love and compassion. It is one of His Great Commandments that we should do unto others only such things as we should want done unto us. In His teaching about the Last Things, He reminds us yet again that whatever we have done, or failed to do, for others, we have done or failed to do, for Him.

We have all been guilty of cruelty at some time or another. We have caused unnecessary suffering, or failed to alleviate such suffering when it was in our power to do so. At the Comprehensive High School where I am Headmaster, I am also the St. John Ambulance Registered First Aider. When our School Nurse is not on duty, pupils with medical or first aid problems tend to gravitate towards my office. I think I am patient and (I hope!) helpful most of the time, but I'm only human (some of my long-suffering pupils and staff would probably say 'less than human'!) and when I am struggling to finish an urgent piece of work before the post goes, and a little cherub in the first year remedial group who is notoriously fond of missing lessons on any pretext comes asking to have a bandage put on what appears to me to be a perfectly sound and healthy wrist or ankle for the third time that week, then perhaps I am neither as patient nor as helpful as I should be. If I am misjudging him and he has a genuine pain, then I am being downright cruel to send him smartly back to his classroom, without his bandage and his sympathy.

We all do it from time to time.

Then there is the terrifying cruelty we read of daily in the Press, or hear about on television news: hooligans who fire crossbows at random into people and animals, indescribably sick criminals and psychopaths who beat up pensioners, women and tiny children; the unspeakable things which terrorists do to their hostages, and the desperately anxious families waiting interminably for their loved ones to be released.

The cruel and their victims are both greatly in need of our prayers.

Prayer

Lord of mercy, it is so easy for us to be cruel and to disguise it even from ourselves. Help us to understand our motives clearly, so that we are never cruel for the sake of it and never try to justify or disguise it with acceptable words like 'painful duty' or 'following the regulations'. Give us a strong and genuine hatred of cruelty in all its forms, so that we shall be among the first to denounce it and fight against it. Fill us with active pity for all victims of cruelty, so that we shall be among the first to alleviate their distress and suffering. Help us to pray for those who are cruel, that their eyes may be opened, as were John Newton's when he turned his back on the cruel traffic in slaves, and became a minister of the Gospel. We ask it for the sake of Him who said "Father, forgive them ... "as He himself suffered terrible cruelty, Jesus Christ our Lord. Amen.

Depression

Thoughts

There are some illnesses — hay fever is one of them, and migraine is another — during which you cannot imagine what it is like *not* to have them. The converse is also true. The hay fever or migraine sufferer who is *not* actually in the grip of a high pollen count or a splitting headache cannot readily bring his unwelcome symptoms vividly to mind. He knows that they are very unpleasant and that he doesn't want them back, but he can't really recapture the precise sensations.

Of all such states, depression is probably the most characteristic. When it has its claws into us, we find it hard to imagine — impossible to imagine — what it is to find life bright, happy and enjoyable. When the depression has lifted, we find it hard to imagine what it was like when we were in it. So fickle are our subjective feelings that they give us a small but useful clue towards understanding how to tackle the problem of depression.

The abject misery of serious, clininical depression is real enough in one sense, yet in another it is insubstantial and ephemeral. The world does not change. Our circumstances do not change. It is our subjective interpretation of that world, our perspective on our circumstances, which fluctuates. The depressed artist can look at his finished canvas and judge it to be a miserable failure when he is in the grip of depression. Three great independent art critics may tell him that it is a masterpiece: in that mood he cannot, he will not, believe them. When his depression has gone, he can look at his canvas and believe it to be a masterpiece against every art critic in the world who is telling him that it is mediocre. The man and the mood have changed: canvas and pigment remain the same.

Prayer

Lord of all hopefulness, Lord of all joy, Lord of all that is truly real, help us to understand our depression for the false and empty deception that it is. Help us, Lord of promise, to see that however we look at our lives and circumstances, all things are in Thy hands, and that all things work together for good in Thy perfect plan. Help us so to understand ourselves that no shadows from our own minds obscure for us the joyful radiance of Thy Presence. We ask it in and through the Name of Him who came to turn our darkness into light, and to bring us the oil of joy for mourning, Jesus Christ our Lord. Amen.

Disappointment, Defeat and Failure

Thoughts

"We lost!"   "They wouldn't give me the mortgage!"

"It didn't work out!"   "I wasn't selected."

"I didn't get the job!"   "I failed!"

And so on, and so on, and so on . . . The list is long and very painful. Failure hurts. Defeat is like a physical blow. Disappointment corrodes the personality. No-one wants to lose. The most stable, balanced and mature of personalities enjoys winning and hates losing.

Yet we learn more from failure than from success. We mature more by riding our defeats and disappointments than we do by winning all the time.

The worst thing to do with failure and disappointment is to brood on it internally. It festers and grows into something singularly vengeful, venomous and alienated. Bring it out. Talk to your friends about it. Tell those who care how you really feel.

Most important of all, talk to God about it. Our Lord Jesus was often disappointed, let down and betrayed. The people He preached to must have disappointed Him. They came to see miracles. They came to be healed. They very rarely took in the full spiritual meaning of what He taught them. His disciples were often a disappointment to Him. In Gethsemane they all forsook Him and fled. Peter, their leader after our Lord's Ascension, once denied with an oath that he even knew Jesus. They argued about who was to be greatest in His Kingdom. Judas, one of the Twelve, betrayed his Master for thirty pieces of silver. Jesus has set us a great example in His prayer life. He took everything to His Father, and He took it often. His disappointments, grievous as they were, never interfered with His work because He took them to His father in prayer. We must learn to do the same.

Prayer

Almighty and everlasting Lord, Your Power never fails; Your sight is never dim; You never leave us nor forsake us. We often fail. We are frequently defeated. We experience disappointment over and over again. Help us not to be cast down by failure; never overthrown by disappointment; nor overwhelmed by defeat. Help us to learn from failure, and to go on again with You to guide and help us. Help us to face our disappointments squarely and live through them. Help us to recover from defeat, always believing that although we may have lost a battle, we have not lost the war. Keep the matchless example of our Lord and Saviour Jesus Christ ever before us, and fill us with the power of Your Holy Spirit so that in coping with failure, defeat and disappointment, we may rise up again strengthened and renewed and ready to try again. We ask it in the Name of Him who forgave the failures of others, but never failed them, Jesus Christ our Lord. Amen.

Disaster

Thoughts

Sooner or later, when there is a disaster, the thought must occur to us in some form or another: how can I reconcile this horror and suffering with a God of Love? It has been argued by some atheists and agnostics that if God exists at all, He cannot be all-powerful and all-loving as we Christians claim He is, in the face of a thousand terrible disasters. If He is all-loving but not all-powerful, then the disaster happens against His will. If He is all-powerful but not all-loving then He could have averted the disaster, but did not wish to do so. It is a difficult problem, but it must be faced squarely and honestly. The matter is too deep and serious for philosophical sophistry or theological prestidigitation.

There are no quick, simple or easy answers. This question is a deadly rock on which many a faith has foundered before now, and will do so again; but foundered faiths have been repaired and refloated in spite of it. Badly crippled vessels have still made their way safely to the Heavenly Harbour with the help of the Divine Pilot.

Ten books of ten times this length would not deal adequately with all the aspects of this great question: but not being able to do much is no excuse for doing nothing at all.

Let us look at a few friendly currents and favourable winds that may improve our chances of getting through these difficult and dangerous waters.

Firstly, we don't know the entire story. We can't see more than a minute fraction of the whole picture. What looks like massive tragedy and unmitigated disaster when seen from earth may not look quite like that from the eternal standpoint. What we call 'death' looks like an ending from here: seen from Heaven it's a beginning. A loss on earth is a gain in Heaven.

Disasters bring agony, suffering, misery and death: they also bring heroism, unselfishness, sacrifice and sympathy of the highest order. No human mind has a yardstick capable of measuring those things. No human hand can hold up the cosmic scales of Infinite Value and weigh life, death and virtue against one another.

This earth is at best a place of preparation for something so much better, so much bigger, and so much more wonderful that we cannot even begin to imagine it. We can get some idea of it from the fact that God's Only Begotten Son, Jesus Christ, was prepared to become a Man, living and dying for us here on earth, in order that we might enjoy with Him forever the delights of the Kingdom of God. No suffering here, however terrible and prolonged, will seem of any significance at all when set against the abundant and everlasting joy of heaven.

Confronted by disaster and the suffering it entails, the man of faith can only admit with Job of old that there are things which a finite human mind, encapsulated in time and space, cannot understand: we may shake our heads in bewilderment as the world seems to disintegrate around us, but through our baffled tears we must still whisper, "I believe . . ."

Would not a God whose ways were totally understood by His creation be somehow less of a God?

And finally there is the huge problem of free will: without real freedom there can be no real love. Our love for God would be meaningless unless we were free to give it or withhold it. If God's loving presence in the universe was always so clearly obvious that there was no room for doubting His Loving Nature or His All-Powerful Will, only a fool could fail to respond to Him. And where would our freedom be then? Is the possibility of disaster one of the coins which we have to hand over in return for a ticket to ride where we choose in the universe?

Prayer

Almighty Father, Your Ways are beyond our understanding: Your Nature and Your Power are further above us than we are able to comprehend; but we know through the revelation of Your Incarnate Son that You are All Love and All Power. Help us to face disaster when it comes with courage and compassion, with self-sacrifice and sympathy: when the worst happens may it bring out the best in us. Keep the glorious example of Your Son our Lord ever before us, that strengthened by Him, and inspired by the Holy Spirit, we may try to face whatever comes as resolutely as He faced the Cross for us. Help all those who suffer death, pain, disability and bereavement because of disaster, and grant us grace to be always ready to help them by word and deed, caring for others as we would have others care for us. We ask it in and through the Name of Him who is our sure Stronghold during all disasters, Jesus Christ our Lord. Amen.

Doubt

Thoughts

Doubt is best understood as one of the roads to faith; the problem is that a road which leads *to* a desirable destination can also lead from it. Everything really depends upon how we choose to use the road.

We use the concept of doubt very figuratively, often adorning it with bouquets of prepositions and adjectives: some things are *beyond* doubt; others are *without* doubt; at times we are *in* doubt. In law we talk about *reasonable* doubt, and there we seem to have have encountered the heart of the matter. Can reason and doubt form such an unexpected emulsion? It is reason which leads us to believe. It is also reason which leads us to doubt. When the sky is heavy with dark, ominous clouds, we have reason to believe that there will soon be heavy rain. When the summer sky is blue and cloudless, and there is scarcely a breath of wind, we have reason to believe that it will be a hot day. To doubt the kind of weather which those conditions indicate is not a reasonable doubt.

Consider the universe around you: think of Beethoven's music; Leonardo's paintings; Wren's architecture; Einstein's mathematics; Shakespeare's dramas; Wordsworth's poetry and Plato's philosophy. Is it reasonable to believe that all of those things just happened *by accident*? Is it reasonable to believe that all their creative genius came from a series of extraordinarily lucky chances which changed a single celled blob of animated jelly into the human race?

Personally, I don't think it's reasonable. I think faith in a Creator is far more reasonable.

It's in all life's important places that doubt, faith and reason meet, and they meet in the same way that molten lava meets the sea. Those who ask God's help to see them through the cataclysmic turmoil of that meeting will find that a breathtaking New Land has been forged from it.

Prayer

God of All Wisdom, Truth and Knowledge, help us to live through the devastating collisions of doubt and faith. Grant us that true and perfect faith which emerges stronger for being tested, and deeper for being tried. Help us ever to remember those saints and heroes of old who came through doubt to a greater and more wonderful knowledge of Thy Truth, and to model our lives upon theirs. Let us like them look ever towards Him whose perfect faith and perfect love redeemed the world, Jesus Christ our Lord. Amen.

Facing Death

Thoughts

La Rochefoucauld once wrote that neither death nor the sun could be looked at steadily, yet the time comes when every man must look: no matter how desperately the eyes and mind beg to turn away.

Death is the great question, the ultimate challenge, and the final mystery.

An anonymous Victorian poet wrote of death:—

'tis the setting of the sun
To rise again tomorrow,
A brighter course to run
Nor sink again in sorrow.

Studdert Kennedy, the magnificent World War I Chaplain, wrote that death *"... was not anything but Satan's lie upon eternal life."* If any man wrote from bitter and multitudinous experience of death, he did.

Christ came to bring us eternal and abundant life: and I believe with absolute certainty that He was truly the Son of God, whose word we can take with complete confidence.

I believe with St John, the Gospel writer, that God so loved the world that He gave His only begotten Son that whosoever believeth on Him should not perish but have everlasting life, and I also believe that in His Father's house are many mansions, and that He has gone ahead to prepare a place for us.

Let's make that simple, direct and personal: God's only Son, our Lord Jesus Christ, came to earth to suffer and die so that we — that is *YOU*, me and everyone who will believe in Him and repent — may live with Him in Heaven in unimaginable joy *forever*.

That is the heart of the Gospel, the quintessence of Truth.

That is the One Great Fact that enables us to live our lives meaningfully, and to die calmly and courageously.

Prayer

Lord of Life and Conqueror of Death, I am walking through the Valley of the Shadow. Be with me. I need You more now than ever before. Forgive me for all that I have ever done wrong, for every sin and every trespass, for every foolish thought and stupid action. Forgive me for listening to the world, when I should have listened only to You. Forgive me for yielding to temptation when I should have prayed for strength to resist it. I am in Your hands now, most merciful Lord. There is nowhere else I can go, for You alone have the words of eternal life. Bring me safely across the dark waters and receive me into Your eternal Kingdom. May those I have loved who have gone before me, be there to welcome me with Your Holy Saints, Angels and Martyrs. Most of all, gracious Lord, may I come to know and serve You in the eternal glory of Your Presence, which is more than any man can ask or deserve. I dare to ask it only because I know that You bid me come. So I commit myself utterly to You, and wait upon Your own good time. I rest upon Your Mercy, in the Name of Christ my Redeemer, in Whom I trust forever and forever. Amen.

Failure to Communicate

Thoughts

Far more of the world's problems than we realise are the result of communication failure.

People don't understand one another.

Many people don't even try to understand one another.

Christ our Lord has told us not to judge. We know only too well how fallible human judgement can be. We apportion blame where there is no blame. We find fault where there is no fault. We criticise what we have no right to criticise because we do not know all the facts, and when we do know all the facts we don't interpret them in the same way as the other person does. We do not always understand ourselves or our own motives very clearly, how much less can we hope to understand other people?

Prayer

Lord of Perfect Wisdom and Complete Knowledge, help us to understand one another better. Help us never to judge our brothers and sisters harshly, for our judgements are often likely to be wrong and unfair. Help us to express our own meanings clearly and courteously, with patience and good humour. Grant us the grace to listen as carefully as possible to others and make every effort to understand them, no matter how great our differences of speech, culture and custom. Lord, in Your infinite wisdom and mercy, You chose to communicate with us by coming to live among us as a Man, so that we could have the best possible opportunity of learning Your message of salvation. Help us to understand that glorious Gospel message, and to respond to it by repenting and following You. We ask it in and through the precious Name of Jesus Christ, who taught the people in parables, and spoke with authority and not as the scribes when He communicated the Truth of the Kingdom of God to men. Amen.

Fear

Thoughts

How many times have my fears turned out to be ill-founded? How often have I dreaded some events: an interview, an examination result, a visit to the doctor or the dentist, only to find that there was nothing to fear at all.

I have heard telephones and trembled inside more wildly than the bell was ringing: and there was no ill news.

I have heard a knock at my door and gone to answer it with leaden feet: and there stood a loving friend with a generous gift.

Sometimes I have felt a tangible fear, so strong that I was almost physically crushed beneath its weight. Sometimes fear has been a lurking shadow in the trees at the edge of a dark and lonely road. Sometimes I think I have been afraid of fear itself. Yet I am still here to talk and write of it. Where fear lurked, God protected. Where fear misled, the Holy Spirit guided back to safety. Where fear paralysed, Christ gave strength.

Jesus teaches us that perfect love casts out fear, and it is a true and wonderful saying.

God made us; God sustains us; nothing can pluck us from His Hand. He loves us with an unconquerable and undying love. He is on our side. He is with us at all times and in all places. How can we have room in our hearts for fear when we are filled with Christ?

Prayer

Lord Jesus, You once walked this earth, as we walk it now. Although You are Very God of Very God, You were once incarnate here, Flesh of our flesh, Man among men. You experienced every temptation that besets us, and You overcame them all. You know how men can feel afraid; your disciples were afraid in the storm on the Lake. Lord, as you helped them, we pray that You will help us now. Saviour, we fear the unknown: but all things are known to You. Teach us to trust You, absolutely and implicitly, in all things, that we may experience Your Perfect Love which casts out fear.

We ask it in and through Your Precious Name. Amen.

Handicap and Disability

Thoughts

There is a scene in the Monty Python comedy about King Arthur in which the belligerent Black Knight challenges the men of Camelot to combat. He loses an arm, but continues the fight shouting, "It's only a flesh wound!" Before the fight is over he has lost all four limbs, but is still shouting defiantly, "Come back here and I'll bite you to death!" Arthur's victorious knights ride away.

Only a far-fetched black comedy, of course, and a zany, off-beat style of humour which is not to everyone's taste. Some of the other scenes and some of the other films are certainly not to mine, but this particular episode featuring The Black Knight has a lot to teach us.

Given a wound that would drive most men from the field without loss of honour, this knight makes light of it and carries on with his impertinent challenges to warriors who have already proved themselves vastly superior to him in combat. This is a kind of cheeky courage which we cannot help but admire.

In *The Entertainer* we see something of the same unsinkable qualities in poor old Archie Rice the unsuccessful music hall comedian who will not give up. He's short on talent, money, integrity, friends . . . But he goes on fighting to stay in show business till the last curtain falls.

Bruce admired it in the spider.

We see it in London sparrows and urban pigeons, risking their lives for crumbs beneath the wheels of buses and taxis.

Cheerfulness is a tremendous defence against incapacity and handicap. In the course of my parish duties I had the pleasure and privilege of calling on a gallant old Churchman in his eighties who lived quite alone and had scarcely enough strength to get out of bed. Yet he was always cheerful, always full of lively and interesting conversation, and certainly full of the love of Christ.

In beds and wheelchairs, on walking frames and sticks, limbless, sightless, deaf and paralysed: they are a gallant and formidable army. Each time I see them, I learn from them. They overcome adversity. They live with their various infirmities and disabilities. Theirs is courage and cheerfulness of the highest order. When they can do nothing else to forward the Kingdom of God, they can still pray for its coming, and inspire the rest of us with their cheerfulness and unconquerable spirits.

God bless the handicapped; they do more for the able-bodied than they themselves can ever know.

Prayer

For the Handicapped

Lord, help me with this disability. Teach me to live cheerfully with my incapacity. Grant me the grace to cope bravely with this infirmity. Lord of healing, I also ask for Your healing touch. Nothing is beyond Your power. I know from the Scriptures that some who had suffered for many years were made whole and strong again by Your Blessed Son, Jesus Christ. Make me strong and well again, Lord. Grant me patience, courage and faith. Help me to smile for the sake of those who tend me and visit me. Help me to think of things to pray for. Give me the names of others who need my prayers, that in the great work of prayer I may labour constantly and steadfastly for You, for the sake of Christ our Saviour. Amen.

For Those Who Love and Care for the Handicapped

All caring and loving Lord, help me to care as You do for those of Your Children who are in extra need of such care. May I never lose patience, or show weariness when they need me; may I always put You first, them second and myself last. Help me to see that it is a special privilege to be called to look after them, and give me the skill to care for them so well that my work will bring happiness and joy into their lives. I ask it in the Name of Christ who cared for us all and gave His life that we might live. Amen.

Humiliation

Thoughts

Nobody likes to be humiliated, ridiculed or made a fool of: yet it happens to most of us from time to time. It happens to the practised public speaker who confidently takes his notes from his dinner-jacket pocket, beams round at the assembled professional men and women sitting at the table in the five star hotel, glances down at his notes and finds that it's the wrong speech. This is the Architects' Dinner. He's brought the speech full of clever little anecdotes and witticisms directed specifically towards the Dental Surgeons. This is not going to be one of his better evenings.

It happens to the Headmaster who can remember most of Shakespeare's plays verbatim when he's giving one of his occasional literary lectures to the Upper Sixth, but who has unfortunately forgotten the name of the Pupil standing in front of him with an outraged parent because an exasperated member of staff has finally clipped the boy's ear.

It happens to the Priest presenting a confirmation candidate to his Bishop, when the name card has fallen off, and the Priest can't remember the girl's name although he's spent the previous two months running the Preparation Class which she faithfully attended.

It happens to us all. It hurts when we go for interview for a job we'd confidently expected to get, only to be passed over in favour of one of our colleagues with fewer qualifications and less experience.

It hurts when we tell that marvellously funny joke we heard on holiday last week . . . and no-one laughs.

It happened to our Lord Jesus Christ Himself in terrible ways: he was mocked by the priests, the scribes, the Sadducees, the Pharisees, the Roman soldiers who plaited the crown of thorns and gave the King of Kings a reed for a sceptre. He was derided and mocked even as He hung dying on the cross. "He saved others. Himself He cannot save."

Christ entered into all our human sufferings, even into mockery, derision and humiliation, so that we could share in His eternal joy.

Prayer

Lord of all dignity, calmness and serenity, help me to deal with humiliation when it comes. Help me to remember how You were mocked and tormented when You came down from Heaven's glory to live in this sad, cruel, savage and uncaring world for my sake. Help me to deal with my own small humiliations by not taking myself too seriously over trivial matters which I imagine affect my status or my position. Remind me, Lord, that the only position which is of any worth is lined up behind You and that the only place to be is following in Your footsteps, and the only status that is of any worth is the eternal status of being a true believer in You. Remind us, Lord, that Your judgement of us is the only judgement that matters, and that the world's laughter is of less consequence than the crackling of thorns on the campfire below a cooking pot. Teach us, Good Lord, that when we are disgraced and humiliated in our own eyes, and in the mocking eyes of the world, in Your all-seeing eyes we are still the child You love. We ask it in the Name of Your Glorious Son, Whose mighty resurrection bewildered and astounded those who had mocked His Divine Kingship, Jesus Christ our Lord. Amen.

Immorality

Thoughts

We fight against the world, the flesh and the devil, and all three are very strong. Some of the foulest poisons have the most alluring packaging. The deadliest drinks at a Borgia banquet were served in the most artistic bottles and glasses. Delilah was neither plain nor homely. Queen Jezebel must have been beautiful as well as evil to have attracted Ahab in the first place.

It must produce much sardonic laughter and mockery in hell when Satan succeeds in perverting and corrupting the beautiful, handsome and attractive men and women whom God has made to enjoy each other's love within the sacred bonds of life-long marriage. Lucifer must derive great satisfaction when ministers of the Church run away with parishioners' wives, bringing heart-break and ruin to two families, and a circle of caring and sorrowing friends. It must give Apollyon a grim smile when he sees the good and natural, God-given, loving desires that a man should have for his wife deflected towards other men, or helpless, innocent children, or some strange fetish or perversion. Beelzebub must chuckle with satisfaction when a man prefers pornography to prayer, blue videos to Bible study, and adultery to adoration.

Whatever the defenders of this sick, decadent, corrupt and permissive society may try to argue, there is only one Christian standard of sexual morality. We may often have failed hopelessly in our efforts to live up to it, but there is no alternative to it which is compatible with true Christianity. A Christian can enjoy sex within marriage and nowhere else, and a marriage is a binding and life-long sacrament joining a man and a woman. Relationships between partners of the same sex are strictly and unequivocally forbidden, so is adultery and any other kind of sex outside marriage.

Like everything else that's worthwhile, it's very difficult indeed, and without God's help it would be totally impossible.

Prayers

Lord of all purity and perfection, You Who made us know us and understand our weaknesses better than we understand ourselves. You know what is good for us, and what is best for us. We only think we know where to find happiness. You know the way to joy beyond our furthest imaginings and You have planned that joy for us forever. Help us never to go astray, never to take what we think we want instead of what is right and good and in accordance with Your Perfect Will. Help us, Lord of the True and Eternal Standards, to live faithfully by Your Standards in the face of every temptation and every lure of the world, the flesh and the devil. We ask it in the Name of Him Who overcame every temptation, and by Whose strength and help we can do the same, Jesus Christ our Lord. Amen.

Imprisonment

Thoughts

When we remember that it is God who gives us the only true liberty through our membership of His Church, the Body of Christ, and that it is His will that we should be free, then we recall how terrible a thing the loss of liberty is.

Yet as the poet writes, "Stone walls do not a prison make, nor iron bars a cage." Jakow Trachtenberg, the brilliantly innovative mathematician who founded the Trachtenberg Institute of Mathematics in Zurich, was a prisoner of the Nazis for many years. He kept his mind free by exploring new concepts and methods of computation, while his body suffered in a concentration camp.

Whatever our circumstances, convict or hostage, prisoner of conscience or criminal serving time for crimes committed, we can free our minds and spirits by turning to the eternal things, and to Christ whose mission to this earth was to bring us freedom from sin and death.

Prayers

Lord Jesus Christ, Son of the living God, You were arrested by the High Priest's soldiers in the Garden of Gethsemane. The King of the Universe was deprived of His liberty by sinful men. Be with all who suffer imprisonment, justly or unjustly, with or without cause. Speak to each captive heart and bring peace and freedom of the spirit to all prisoners. Help those who have sinned and committed crimes to repent and wait patiently for proper legal liberty. Help and bless all who guard them, and minister to them as Prison Chaplains. Grant that those who have lost their liberty through no faults of their own may be swiftly set free. We ask it for the sake of Him Who came to free captive humanity, and became a captive Himself that we might be free from sin and death, Jesus Christ our Lord. Amen.

Mental Illness and Breakdown

Thoughts

Sometimes things have to be broken before they can be restored. A skilful surgeon has to re-break a leg that has been badly set before he can straighten and re-set it to make it true, strong and whole again.

A failing business has to be wound-up, and its assets sold, before what's been salvaged can be used to start a new and prosperous enterprise.

Sometimes a mind is overwhelmed by grief, anxiety or stress. There is more pressure than it can cope with, and it has to break down before it can be restored.

The world is full of living parables of breakdown and re-birth. Old vegetation falls into the earth and new crops grow. A corn of wheat falls into the ground and 'dies' and from its 'death' a new plant is born that bears a hundredfold.

It takes the bravest of riders to remount a horse that has thrown him, the bravest of entrepreneurs to start again after his business has failed.

Think of a mental illness, or a breakdown, not as a crippling and permanent failure but as a wonderful opportunity for the mind to start again and succeed.

Prayers

Lord, of compassion, the floods swept over me and carried me away, but You heal and restore me. I have passed through fire and storm, and travelled in strange and desolate places, but You heal and restore me. I have been alone, angry, perplexed, bewildered and frightened. I have sometimes lost my grip on reality and even on myself, but You heal and restore me. As the potter remakes the clay that has twisted into the wrong shape, remake me, O loving and supremely skilful Master Craftsman. From these ruins make me anew, that I may serve You faithfully and well, forever and forever. I ask it for the sake of Him Who healed all sicknesses of mind and body when He walked this earth as a Man, and still heals and restores today, Jesus Christ our Lord. Amen.

Old Age

Thoughts

In Norse mythology there is a story of Thor, their great warrior-god, being tricked by the Frost Giants. He challenges them to wrestle with him, but is told that he must first have a contest with their old nurse. To his amazement and humiliation, this apparently feeble and infirm old woman defeats him after a long and bitter struggle. It is not until after he has left the Giants' Hall that they reveal the truth to him: the 'old nurse' is Old Age who must at last bring the greatest warrior to his knees.

There is no shame in being defeated by an enemy who can bring down even the Champion of Asgard. Yet the myth has more to teach us than that: the image of the old nurse is significant. Age is not entirely our enemy: there are comforts and compensations in it. In our vigorous prime we are in danger of being arrogant, feeling too strong and self-sufficient to need help from God or man. A warrior's character can be improved more by an occasional defeat than by a string of uninterrupted victories. Sometimes it is as noble to accept help graciously as to give it generously. Old age gives us time to think, to reflect, to meditate and to pray: these are sometimes more important than working and doing. And prayer comes into both categories: it is the most important and productive work of all.

Prayers

Lord of all life and of every age. You have protected and guided me since before I was born. Everything I am and everything I have ever done is known to You. From childhood to manhood, You have been with me, even in those places where I turned away from Your love and sinned against You. Forgive me, most merciful Lord, and grant me an inward assurance of Your forgiveness. Let me know the reality of Your pardon and peace within. I give my remaining years to You. Lead me step by step and day by day, as You have always done. Find me some task in Your service that is still within my strength. Find me some lonely soul to whom I can yet bring Your gift of companionship; find me some hungry soul whom I can yet feed with the Bread of Heaven; find me some thirsty soul to whom I can bring the Water of Life; find me some lost soul to whom I can still show the Way. I ask it in the Name of Christ, my Lord and Saviour. Amen.

Lord, give me strength to battle on relentlessly against the pain and weariness that comes with age. As each task grows harder and heavier with the passing years, give me a will of steel to discipline my wandering thoughts, and to make this intermittent memory report for duty when I need it. Give me a will that can never be defeated by aching limbs or a struggle for breath. Give me the heart of a Christian warrior still eager for the battle when Christ's trumpet calls, no matter how slowly these old hands now buckle armour and draw their sword. Never let me forget that even the oldest Christian soldier can still defend his appointed place on the walls of Jerusalem. Grant me this, God of all power and might, for the sake of Your Son, whose unbreakable will withstood the very worst pains and hardships, and overcame death that I might live, Jesus Christ our Lord. Amen.

Pain

Thoughts

It can be very slight, caused by something as trivial as a tiny splinter or an accidental encounter with the point of a sewing needle. It can be the much sharper, deeper and acuter stab of a nerve below a tooth. It can be the searing agony of a severe burn, the prolonged and excruciating pains of trapped nerves, of rheumatism or of arthritis.

At one time or another almost all of us have experienced pain in various forms and degrees of severity. Some pains begin with an unbearable explosive force that threatens to overwhelm us in that same instant, then, after long desperate hours, they gradually subside until they can be tolerated. Others begin as a vague discomfort or a dull, scarcely definable ache. Hour by hour they grow steadily worse, gaining their insidious hold over mind, action and will until it seems the pain has become master of the man.

Christ knew all about pain. Because it is among the worst of all human experiences, He drank its bitter cup to the dregs for our sakes.

When we ourselves are desperate with pain, we can turn to Him for help secure in the knowledge that He understands every atom of it. He Himself has travelled that road for us. He knows what we are going through, and He cares more deeply for us than we care for ourselves.

Prayer

All conquering and triumphant Lord, help me to bear this pain, to come through it, and to conquer it, with Your help. Lord of all strength, all courage and all fortitude, grant me a sufficient portion of Your courage to enable me to endure this present pain honourably and with dignity. Inspire me with Your example and grant me victory over it. Lord of all gentleness and tenderness, compassion and sympathy, in Your great mercy take this pain from me. Grant me Your peace and tranquillity, Your calmness, quietness and rest, Your healing, wholeness and restoration, for Your Name's sake, Amen.

Perplexity

Thoughts

Things are very rarely straightforward, clear-cut, or black and white. There are many shades of grey. A very light grey is almost indistinguishable from white, and a very dark grey is almost indistinguishable from black, yet in the centre of the scale there are mid-greys so similar that they are almost indistinguishable from one another.

It is when we are trying to sort out these middle greys that we run into difficulties which bewilder and perplex us. There is another huge paradox here.

Christianity is a revealed religion. It is not the product of human minds. It is the truth which God has revealed to us over the centuries through his priests and prophets, and which reaches its fullness in the Incarnation of our Lord and Saviour Jesus Christ, who is both Perfect God and Perfect Man. As a revealed religion Christianity cannot recognize shades of grey. We are either for God or for Satan. There is no comfortable fence on which we can sit. There is no half-way house in which we can lodge.

But one glance at any real moral question of any depth tells us that there *are* shades of grey. Should a Christian be a warrior or a pacifist? A fair case can be made, and is made, by honest, sincere, thinking Christians of both persuasions. I would use force — ultimate force if necessary — to stop a criminal, or a crazy politician like Hitler, from injuring or killing a helpless and innocent victim. There are other Christians who tell me with equal sincerity that they would not. I cannot judge between us. I can only follow what I believe to be the true and correct interpretation. And that, hopefully, resolves our paradox of perplexity. It is not the faith that has grey areas: it is man's interpretation and understanding that is at fault. God's truth is there: in Law, in Prophecy, in the Gospels and in the Church. If ten visitors to an art gallery go there to study a Masterpiece, and each has a different visual handicap — one is short-sighted, another is colour-blind, and so on — each will give a different account of the Masterpiece he has been studying. Each in his own way is telling the truth, yet his imperfect sight separates his version from that of his companions. The Masterpiece itself, of course, remains perfect and unimpaired by the faulty vision of its observers.

Prayer

Dear Lord, I am often perplexed and bewildered. I find the world a difficult place to understand at times. You have all truth, wisdom and knowledge within Yourself. You are the Way, the Truth and the Life. We cannot come to You unless we come by You, and we know that You have bidden us to come. Blessed Lord, forgive our folly, our blindness, our quarrelling and our argumentativeness. Help us to concentrate upon loving and serving You, rather than fighting amongst ourselves. When we are in the dark, shed Your Light upon us. When we are lost, send Your Holy Spirit to guide us. When we are perplexed, clear our minds with Your Truth, for the sake of the Living Truth, Jesus Christ our Lord. Amen.

Sickness

Thoughts

When we are brought low by sickness, when illness takes our strength and energy, when we tremble and shake with fever, when we shiver with the unnatural coldness that accompanies some illnesses, it is hard to remember what radiant health should be like.

Some of us have never known the dynamic fitness and energy of good health. Illness has shadowed us since the day we were born.

Some of us have been ill for many years: our bodies have been weary prisons instead of the instruments of joy and happiness, movement and merriment that they should be.

Miracle is not an empty word. Miracles are not restricted to Bible times. They still happen today. Not even the wisest and most experienced doctor can be 100% certain of anything. Diagnoses and prognoses are only estimates and probabilities: the most trusted and reputable medical experts can be *wrong* —gloriously and wonderfully wrong. Despair is a more certain killer than the most virulent disease. Never believe the pessimists who say that nothing can be done. There is always hope. If the chance is less than one in a thousand million, it is still better than no chance at all. Believe in it! Go for it! There are still divine healings today that baffle the specialists.

Look at the power of the will: it is infinitely greater than we can imagine. Mind has far more control over matter than most of us will dare to allow ourselves to believe: start daring today — tomorrow may be your miracle.

If the power of mere human will is so enormous, what about the Divine Power? That is truly limitless. If some men have achieved the apparently impossible by believing sufficiently in themselves, how much more can we achieve by believing in God?

Prayer

Lord of Health and Wholeness, I feel ill. Help me to marshal all my physical and mental resources to fight this sickness with the help of doctors and nurses, family and friends. Help me to feel the power of the prayers of my loved ones acting upon me like medicine. Give me faith, Lord, in the self-healing powers of my own mind and body. Strengthen my will to live, and my determination to recover. Above all, Greatest of Healers, grant me Your help. All things are possible with You. Drive this illness from me and restore me to health, wholeness and vigour, then give me grace to use that new life in Your service, for the sake of Jesus Christ who healed all kinds of illness and infirmity. Amen.

Stress

Thoughts

In the world of physics there are limits to the amount of stress which a particular object can sustain before it breaks.

When I was employed in the timber industry years ago we had skilled craftsmen who worked as stress-graders. They studied each piece of wood carefully and then decided by its appearance, the closeness of its grain, the number of knot-holes in a given area, and so on, how much stress it could take. Only the strongest timbers were used for such vital things as scaffold boards. Poor quality, unreliable wood was used for cheap, rough packing cases. Later on a stress-grading machine with a computer to control it took the place of the visual grading by craftsmen. Even the best men and the most reliable machines occasionally went wrong: a piece of wood that seemed strong failed under stress.

Some structures which can endure enormous stresses and pressures in one direction will fail under comparatively tiny stresses in another. Structures, materials and men all seem to have their Achilles' heels. There is a chink in the strongest armour. The fictional Superman was weakened by kryptonite. The historical Samson fell because of Delilah's treachery. Robert Service's poem "Fighting Mac" tells of a famous and gallant hero, disgraced by some unknown sin or crime, who commits suicide because of it. "Eyes that could smile at death," wrote Service, "could not face shame."

Where an unsupported, unreinforced structure fails, the building that is braced and buttressed stands firm. The weakest Christian can be strengthened by God to a degree which in his normal, feeble human state he finds almost unbelievable. Our problems with stress arise when we are up against those particular difficulties to which we are most vulnerable, and when we neglect to seek God's help through prayer, the reading of Scripture, worship, Christian fellowship, and sharing in the Blessed Sacrament.

Prayer

Lord Jesus Christ, You endured more stress for our sakes than we can ever hope to understand. With gallant and unfailing courage You bore the agony and humiliation of the cross to achieve our redemption. Be with us, Lord and Master of that stress beyond our imaginings, so that in our passing moments of stress and tension we do not fail You, nor our high calling as Your followers. Inspire us by Your great example: fill us with the Holy Spirit: reinforce us with divine Grace: encourage us with the Heavenly Promises and bring us through our present stress into the calmness and peace of everlasting light and joy with You. We ask it in and through Your precious Name. Amen.

Tension

Thoughts

Just as worry and anxiety are closely related, so too are stress and tension, yet they also have their individual characteristics — there are distinct areas in which each displays its own singular kind of nastiness.

Tension often exists in human relationships. We have all had the experience of working with people, or of sharing family life with people, who could create tension simply by entering the room. It isn't what they do or say as they enter, it's just our awareness that there is likely to be trouble once they've arrived. Various bosses, sergeants, foremen, chargehands, inspectors and similar officials seem to bring an ethos of tension with them when they appear.

Then there are people with whom we get on well enough when we're with them in a one to one situation, but who create tension when other people arrive. The 'professional' peacemakers and negotiators of industry and the Diplomatic Corps are well aware of this when they act as go-betweens between parties who are at loggerheads with each other. If they can see the warring individuals separately — for at least part of the negotiation — it simplifies the task of reconciling them.

It isn't only people who create tension: sometimes it's the situation in which the people find themselves. They might have got on very well if they'd met at Church, at work, or at a party. They don't find a wet road surface, a dangerous intersection and two crumpled cars conducive to friendly relations. Two girls interested in the same eligible man — and vice versa — are in a tension-generating environment. Seven long-term unemployed waiting to be interviewed for one job are in a difficult social situation. The personnel officer who has to come in at the end and give the verdict is likely to feel very tense about that situation, especially if he's a caring and sensitive person.

Emotional and mental conflicts generate tension; so do ambivalent feelings. There are some things which both attract and repel us at the same time. We may be desperately tempted towards some particular sin, know it to be a sin, and find it almost impossibly hard to resist the temptation. During that period of struggle we are in a state of tension. We may be keen to apply for a promotion, but hate the interviewing and selection processes through which we must pass on the way: the desire for the promotion and the dislike of the interviews, or the fear of the subsequent dis-appointment if we're not successful, create tension.

Some psychologists and psychiatrists have suggested that within reasonable boundaries tension may even be good for us: we don't have to agree with their findings, and it's probably a thing that varies enormously with individuals. One man shrugs off a degree of tension that gives his neighbour a nervous breakdown. Whether our individual breaking point is high or low, and whether small amounts of tension may be good for us or not, it is undeniable that too much tension is dangerous and destructive for anyone. It is when we feel ourselves getting close to that warning level that we need the Divine Help more than ever.

Prayer

Almighty God, Creator and Sustainer of our great universe in which men and machines, minds and material things all experience tension of one kind or another, help us to understand what You require of us, and to distinguish worthwhile and necessary effort from futile tension and harmful stress. May we have the strength of steel in our resistance to temptation: the hardness of flint in our defence of what is good and right; and the steadfastness of granite in our refusal to compromise with evil or the fanciful changes of the times. Grant us the firmness of solid rock that we may always put the Spirit of God before the spirit of the age. We ask it through the Name of Him who remained strong, true and dedicated to Your will through all those tensions of mind and spirit which He endured, Jesus Christ, our Warrior Priest, who overcame death that we might live. Amen.

Uncertainty and Indecision

Thoughts

"How long halt ye between two opinions?" thundered the prophet of old.

"A man who is a neutral in this fight is not a man: he's bulk and body without breath ... he makes me sick," wrote Studdert Kennedy.

We live in an age of moral compromise, uncertain ethics and cautious indecision. We need to ask God for the courage to stand up and be counted when it's necessary. We need leaders who are in no doubt about what's right and what's wrong and are not afraid to say so.

There's one kind of indecision and uncertainty which is not strictly intellectually honest, but is often practised because it is politically expedient, economically advantageous or just simply tactful and diplomatic. We do know really, but in the particular circumstances in which we're asked we'd rather hedge than make a direct, simple and unequivocal statement. The persistant suitor who keeps on asking whether the girl will marry him may be unattractive to her. There is no way that she would say 'yes' in a thousand years, but she makes gentle, tactful answers rather than giving a hard, direct 'no'. If the man concerned is able to take a hint, he will quietly cease asking without causing further difficulty or embarrassment to either of them. To give an uncertain but vaguely discouraging answer in these circumstances may be kindness, cowardice or a gentle reluctance to hurt or disappoint someone. We are invited to an event we don't want to attend. We don't usually say 'no' in a blunt and definite way because it seems both hurtful and discourteous. We usually say, "I'll have to consult my diary. I'll let you know." The show business version after an audition is the infamous, "Don't call us: we'll call you!"

Then there is the other kind of uncertainty and indecision: the genuine kind. There are a number of roads before us. We have several possibilities available. Which do we choose? We should, of course, ask the other and far more important question, the one that really matters. *"Lord, You know all things and You have my true welfare and eternal happiness at heart: please will You show me the way and help me to travel in it?"* A man may be certain that God has called him to the Priesthood, but much less certain about the exact place in which God wants him to exercise that ministry. Should I, for example, stay where I am now as a non-stipendiary Priest and a Headmaster, trying to witness for Christ in a State School as well as in the Church? Should I seek full-time work in a Parish? What about being a School Chaplain in a Christian School? Hospital work? The Prison Chaplaincy? The Armed Services? Am I being called to retire early from School and spend more time writing Christian literature? Should I apply to do a Ph.D. in some branch of research with a Christian context? In the one small life I know better than most, I have a great deal of uncertainty and indecision, a great many things I can't make my mind up about. How many uncertainties do you have to contend with?

The same answer is applicable to us all. We must take the problem to God our Heavenly Father and say as Christ our Lord said, "Not my will, but Thine, be done."

Prayer

Lord, I am often hopelessly indecisive. Sometimes I really don't know what to do or where to go next. I weigh up the pros and cons of the various paths that seem to lie before me, and I have great difficulty in deciding which is best. Preserve me, Lord, from the consequences of my own ignorance, folly and impetuousness. Save me from sloth and greed, from laziness and selfishness. Show me not the path I think I want, but the path I know You want, and then grant me the strength to follow it to the end. We ask it for the sake of Him who went all the way to Calvary for us, Jesus Christ our Lord. Amen.

Vandalism and Violence

Thoughts

Does anyone really *know* why they do it? They destroy beautiful flowers and trees. They cripple and torment defenceless animals. They attack people they've never seen before viciously and savagely. They are atavistic and iconoclastic: like the thief in St. John's Gospel, they enter the sheepfold only to steal, to kill and to destroy. *Do they themselves know why?* Perhaps they don't. Psychologists, psychiatrists and social workers try to tell us that these wild and dangerous youngsters have had difficult backgrounds and unhappy home lives, that they are poor and underprivileged, that they are protesting in the only way they can against what they see as a glossy, uncaring, prosperous and materialistic society that has somehow shut them out from all the good things which it happily distributes among the 'successful' — that is those who know the rules of the financial and materialistic game and use them to maximum advantage.

Yet there have been countless boys and girls from necessitous homes who did very well for themselves, became prosperous and law-abiding pillars of society, and never wrote one word on a wall, nor injured any other human being. Of course it's harder to make good from an underprivileged and necessitous background, but it's far from impossible. We must look deeper than that for the causes of vandalism and violence.

It is moral education and good discipline that have declined at roughly the same rate as the standards of behaviour in our society as a whole. As child-centred permissiveness has grown in more and more homes and schools, so vandalism and violence have increased. Society has lost its moral backbone, its hard skeleton of discipline and order. It has therefore become a jellyfish, and jellyfish sting viciously and indiscriminately.

The Scriptures teach unequivocally that it is the duty of a good father to discipline his children firmly for their own sakes. Until we get back to the security of the well disciplined family and the well disciplined school, violence and vandalism will go on increasing.

Prayer

Almighty God, our Heavenly Father, whose ordering brought the universe out of chaos in the beginning, help us all to see the need for proper law and order in our society. We pray that the tide may turn in our homes and in our schools, that young people themselves, as well as their teachers and parents, may see the need for good order and discipline and learn to welcome it and respect it. Clear the minds of our politicians and other leaders of society that they may see the need for restoring law and order in homes and schools, that violence and vandalism may cease and that society shall be peaceful and orderly. Clear the minds of parents and teachers that they may influence the young people in their care in the right way. Protect all potential victims of violence: the weak, the elderly, the handicapped and the helpless. Defend all good, beautiful and innocent things from the destructiveness and cruelty of vandals, and help us all to play our part in making the world a safer and better place. We ask it for the sake of Jesus Christ our Lord, who drove out of the Temple those who defiled and spoiled it. Amen.

War

Thoughts

Take a steel basin the size of a planet; fill it with guns, bombs, bayonets, grenades and poisonous chemicals. Throw in a few battalions of infantry, a squadron of fearless men on horseback, a flotilla of warships with crew, singing gamely as they sail into battle, gliders full of steel-eyed airborne commandos, and a padre to pray over the dying and write the letters home to their families. Let this terrifying mixture effervesce for a few decades. Modernise the weapons occasionally, and change the political leaders every five years. The product is called war, and it is one of the worst things men have yet devised to do to one another.

One of the worst, not the *very* worst.

Surrendering to tyranny is worse. Standing by and doing nothing while the weak and the helpless, the innocent and the defenceless are enslaved and tortured, raped and massacred is infinitely worse — at least that's my personal verdict.

War is terrible. It is an insane waste of life and human resources. We should do *almost* anything to avoid it, but not *quite* anything. Some things are worse than death. Some horrors are worse than war.

Prayer

Lord of Peace, deliver us from war. May nations live with one another in harmony, justice and friendship, respecting one another and the rights of their citizens.

Lord of Justice, deliver us from the error of peace-at-any-price, and teach us instead to treasure righteousness at any cost.

Lord of Love, help us to live with one another on this world You have given us with understanding, tolerance and mutual respect. Help us to see You in all our fellow men, and love Your Image as we see it in them. Bring us all together into the one great family of God, through the redeeming work of Your Son, our Saviour Jesus Christ. Amen.

Worry

Thoughts

Worry is one of the least productive and most frustrating of all our human activities. As infants in our parent's arms, while we are still too young to know what it is we are worrying about, I suspect that worry has its insidious roots. Is mother there? Why is it dark? I am cold. I am alone. I am too hot. Who are all these people? I am hungry. Will I be fed soon?

We worry about our first day at school. We worry about the teachers, the other children, the lessons we are learning. We worry about changing schools as we grow older. We worry about moving house and losing all our friends. We worry about examinations and tests, about girlfriends, about spots and hairstyles and fashionable clothes. We worry about our health. Some of us become hypochondriacs. Some of us develop phobias. The great majority of us become at least mildly neurotic about something before we escape from the hazards of our teenage years.

Later on we are concerned about our careers, about money, about human relationships. We are worried about nuclear war, radiation, environmental pollution, economic recession, AIDS and a thousand other horrors.

Not one act of worrying has the slightest positive influence on the horrors themselves. Worry reduces our mental efficiency, and takes up time that could profitably be spent in prayer, in worship, in meditation upon the Divine, or in performing acts of service for God and man.

Logic is a useful defence against worry: if a thing is benign or harmless there is no need to worry about it; if it is harmful or evil, and it is within our power to act against it, then let us carry out that action as soon as possible; if it is too vast for us to deal with alone, then let us do what little we can and commit the rest to God in prayer and complete trust.

Humour is also a useful defence against worry. When we hold our worries up to the merciless light of ridicule, they often look foolish and preposterous. The man who has the courage, wisdom and maturity to laugh at himself usually finds that worry has little power over him.

Worry is a creature of dusky corridors, creeping shadows and darkened rooms with their doors ajar. It is ethereal. It tricks us out of our present moment. It cheats and swindles us with unpleasant memories and their possible consequences. It deceives us with visions of possible futures, all of which are unwelcome, humiliating or downright terrifying.

It is God's will that we should enjoy the here and the now, the magical, eternal Present, our preview of eternal and abundant life of Heaven. Worry about the past and the future is only one of Satan's spiteful interventions: an attempt to separate us from the Joy that Christ offers without end and without limit. Worry is the cracked and grimy jug with which Satan attempts to bail out the Ocean of Divine Love.

Prayer

Ever loving Lord, You have taught us so often not to

worry, not to be anxious, and not to be afraid, yet we are slow to learn, and slow to trust You as we should. Forgive us for all our past sins, and reassure us that they are gone forever through the Precious Blood of Christ, so that we need worry over them no more. Teach us to look forward to all that lies ahead, without worry, without anxiety, without distress, for all things are in Your all-loving and all-powerful hands. Remind us, Father, that nothing can ever separate us from the Love of Christ, Your only begotten Son, so that we may always be aware of His loving Presence with us. Reassure us that the Holy Spirit, the Strengthener, Comforter and Inspirer of all who truly seek Him is with us too. We ask it in and through the Name of Jesus, our Redeemer. Amen.